UNDERSTANDING
Jefferson & Justice

America's Misunderstood Founder & Founding

Frank N. Mitchell

This UNDERSTANDING booklet is part of a series
of booklets on key issues of our time on the Reign of
Christ at
www.ashiningcityonahill.org
www.reignofchrist.org
All booklets are available at amazon.com

October 2018

Introduction
to this
Special Edition
for the
2018 Midterm Elections
***

WWJD
What would Jefferson do?

What would Thomas Jefferson say about the upcoming 2018 Midterm Elections and how would he vote? The answer to these questions might be seen as unclear by some but **only** because no American founding figure is more misunderstood today than Thomas Jefferson. Why is this?

In my experience, few people bother to investigate what Jefferson **actually** said, wrote or thought. Modern atheist and Liberal education has created a caricature of Thomas Jefferson, and most people learn this **false** "Jefferson," and then they repeat their misunderstanding without realizing that it is, in fact, a false narrative they have learned about him.

As I explain in this booklet, Jefferson was in fact what we today would call a conservative, though he might be called a "liberal," as the word was used in the 19th century to mean rights for the individual.

However, rights for the individual are today actually associated with conservative positions and not with the Liberal position of today's Democratic Party.

Today, it is *only* the Republican Party that consistently supports individual rights and freedoms across the board based on Thomas Jefferson's moral "Laws of Nature and of Nature's God" as expressed in the Declaration of Independence.

It is only these moral Laws of Nature that can give us the Liberty and Justice for all that we all so long to see once again in America. For its part, for a variety of reasons, the Democrat Party has in recent decades come to advocate a Social Justice agenda that is **the very opposite of everything that Jefferson stood for**, and stood for as the foundational purpose of his public and private life, but few people today know or understand this.

What does this mean? Thomas Jefferson would not only vote *for* every Republican candidate, he would go out of his way to vote *against* every Democrat candidate. There is no other conclusion one can draw if one studies what Jefferson actually believed, wrote, and advocated. Quite simply, Thomas Jefferson would have one important and urgent message for us today in this hour of the 2018 Midterm Elections: **VOTE REPUBLICAN**.

Vote Republican as if your life depended upon it because, in truth, the life of our dear Republic does.

UNDERSTANDING
Jefferson & Justice
America's Misunderstood
Founder & Founding

There is probably no figure in America's founding and in America's founding vision more important than Thomas Jefferson, and there is probably no figure in America's founding more misunderstood today than Thomas Jefferson. In fact, understanding correctly what Thomas Jefferson actually did and said in America's founding is probably the key to solving almost all of the social, political, economic, and education problems of our time.

The Laws of Nature and of Nature's God
The key to understanding America's founding as well as Jefferson himself is the phrase in the Declaration of Independence that speaks of "the Laws of Nature and of Nature's God." These Laws are not the **scientific** Laws of Nature but the **moral** Laws of Nature, Laws which deal with Justice and Righteousness. They are called the Natural Law or the Higher Moral Law, and though few Christians seem to know this, this Law has little to do with Christian salvation, as such, besides revealing by our natural conscience an absolutely perfect moral standard of God that we all fall short of.

America as established in the Declaration of Independence, as well as the Just state more generally, is founded on the moral "Laws of Nature and of Nature's God," and when these Laws are Wisely done in Justice for the good of the whole nation as a commonwealth, this is called statesmanship. This concept of statesmanship comes out of ancient Greek philosophy, and it is a central part of the teachings of Plato, Aristotle, and Cicero. And this idea of statesmanship is implicitly developed in the Bible in the Proverbs, the Old Testament Prophets, and the Psalms.

Technically, statesmanship has little if anything to do with Christian salvation, as such. Statesmanship is a Greek philosophical concept of the moral Laws of Nature which **the Christian has a moral duty to do** as a good legislator or executive. Statesmanship is God's will for government, and it involves doing what is good for the whole nation as opposed to good for special interest groups. True theists, Christian and otherwise, have a moral duty before God to do statesmanship or, that is, what is good for the whole country.

Thomas Jefferson and Deism
Thomas Jefferson as well as Benjamin Franklin both appear to be quite clearly non-Trinitarian Christians. This is a particular form of "Deism" which most people, in my experience, are not familiar with. There are, in fact, two very different types of Deism.

First, there is a Deism as we usually think of it and as it is usually encountered in the literature, and this

Deism is essentially an atheism with a Creator God who creates a clockwork universe and walks away never to be seen or heard from again. This could be called a standard Deism which most people are familiar with, and it does *not* believe in the Higher Moral Law of the "Laws of Nature and of Nature's God" in the first place in order to found a life or country on them in the second place.

This **standard Deism** also does *not* believe in a general inspiration of Scripture *nor* in a life after death *nor* in the righteous intervention of God in history (as Jefferson did) *nor* in the power of prayer (as Franklin did). In fact, Jefferson and Franklin believed in the inspiration of Scripture, life after death, etc., and famously so no less, and **this is what creates another second form of Deism**, which is essentially a non-Trinitarian Christianity.

This second form of Deism holds that God did indeed create a clockwork universe, but He did *not* walk away after He did so, in fact just the opposite!!! This second form of Deism holds that God is quite active in the affairs of men, history, and nations. Franklin famously believed in the power of prayer, and Jefferson famously believed that God would judge America for slavery, which He did with the Civil War.

Sir Isaac Newton is famously also said to have believed in this second form of Deism, and he, accordingly, spent endless hours trying to decipher the book of Revelation! Newton was not very successful in his efforts, but that is beside the point. Newton clearly thought the book of Revelation was the key to understanding history and God's active involvement in it, which is something that a standard Deism firmly rejects as a central tenet of its Deism.

And, more importantly, the second form of Deism (of Jefferson and Franklin) holds the Bible to be the greatest inspired work of moral instruction ever written, completely apart from the more controversial issue of Biblical inerrancy as such. And this second form of Deism believes Jesus to be the greatest moral teacher who ever lived.

All of these things from the power of prayer to God's Righteous judgment in history to the great moral teachings of Jesus are rejected not only by a standard Deism as we think of that term but also by today's Liberals and atheists, who **also** do **not** believe in any of these things as a very central point of their Liberalism and atheism!

The "Jefferson Bible"
It is only the traditional theist (Christian and otherwise) who believes in the Higher Moral Law to be Wisely done for the good of the whole country by the good legislator in order for him to be a true statesman.

Jefferson actually held the moral teachings of Jesus to be unsurpassed, and he, therefore, cut the miracles and various religious passages out of the Gospels in order to create a Natural Moral Law handbook for right living and for doing good legislation and for doing good statesmanship for the common good based on the Higher Moral Law, which probably has no greater exponent than Jefferson besides Jesus himself.

Jefferson's famous version of the Gospels and of the life and teachings of Jesus is often called the "Jefferson Bible." In it Jefferson takes the Gospels, and he cuts out the supernatural events in the Gospels, thus leaving an unsurpassed moral handbook for personal living and happiness as well as for doing good legislation.

In fact, according to Wikipedia and numerous other sources, throughout almost the entire first half of the 20th century, all incoming Congressmen and Senators were given a Jefferson Bible when they first went to Washington in order to have good instruction on making good laws for Justice and Righteousness for the common good based on the moral teachings of Jesus.

In truth, returning to the moral teachings of Jesus (that is, the "Jefferson Bible") as the standard or plumb line for all legislation will probably solve most if not all our problems in Washington DC as it will solve the problems for good government generally in any nation. In fact, almost certainly it is Jefferson's view of good government and good statesmanship that will mark the coming millennium in all nations as theories of Liberalism, atheism, and Social Justice are discredited and fall to the wayside.

The University of Virginia
Further and also famously, in founding the University of Virginia Jefferson maintains a two track approach to education, namely, the school was *not* to resolve theological issues concerning Christian salvation (that is the role of the churches), but rather the school was to teach the moral Laws of Nature and of Nature's God as facts of Nature along with the physical sciences. Again, by contrast, today's Liberals and atheists and many educators do *not* believe in the moral Laws of Nature and of Nature's God, but rather they believe *only* in the physical sciences. Clearly, this was *not* Jefferson's view.

One can only conclude that teaching the moral "Laws of Nature and of Nature's God," the foundation of Jefferson's America and the Declaration of Independence, was presumably **one of the central reasons for Jefferson's founding of the University of Virginia**, though today, as with most universities, this is probably no longer central to that school, if it exists at all as a purpose for the University of Virginia.

A heartbroken Jefferson must look down from heaven and weep at the current state of his school. Again, all of this has little to do with Christian salvation as such, which is a separate issue of individual personal belief in Jesus and his atoning work, which is specifically not part of the Natural Revelation and its moral Laws.

However, all of this means most if not all of America's **political *and* education** problems will be solved by returning to Jefferson's view of the moral Laws of Nature and of Nature's God as central not only to good government but to good education as well. The practical reality of this today is *only* people of the traditional Christian and Jewish faiths are receptive to this idea, while all Liberals and atheists categorically oppose the moral Laws of Nature and of Nature's God of Jefferson and the founders as a central point of their Liberalism and atheism, just as the standard Deists of America's founding did.

This means as a practical matter in order to have people receptive to Jefferson's view of government, statesmanship, education, and the moral Laws of Nature and of Nature's God, we probably have to get vast numbers of people saved in Christ because atheists and Liberals will *never* accept Jefferson's views on government, statesmanship, education, and the moral Laws of Nature and of Nature's God.

Jefferson's *actual* Religion
Jefferson's *actual* religion is often debated and almost always misunderstood. In fact, this writer has never heard of or encountered anyone who knows

what Jefferson's religion was. Jefferson clearly did not like a lot of formal religion for various reasons, and he appears as Franklin to have had little if any interest in salvation issues.

Having said this, just as Franklin did, Jefferson stated what his very strong religious views were, and they are the second form of Deism we looked at above. Again, this is a non-Trinitarian Christianity of believing in God and moral virtue and life after death and a judgment of God after death based on the moral or immoral life one has lived.

There is *no* **ambiguity** about this because Jefferson, as Franklin, went out of his way to tell people his religious views. Jefferson's religion as he states it himself is: "The doctrines of Jesus are simple, and tend all to the happiness of man. 1.) There is only one God, and he is all perfect. 2.) There is a future state of rewards and punishments. 3.) To love God with all thy heart and thy neighbor as thyself, is the sum of religion."

Clearly from this statement, **Jefferson is definitely *not* a modern religious Liberal or atheist**, and it is total revisionist history to claim he is either, though I have rarely if ever encountered a Liberal or atheist who did not think Jefferson was one of them in some form of atheism or Liberalism.

Jefferson was not only an open and self-professed follower of Christ for personal living and for true happiness but for doing statesmanship in Justice and Righteousness in government, which is God's will for government. In doing true statesmanship, it is hard to beat Jefferson, but you will probably need to get out your Jefferson Bible!

Why is there no "Christianity" or "Deism" of a Newton, Franklin or Jefferson today?
Given what we have seen so far, a very reasonable and obvious question tends to emerge: Why is there no "Christianity" or "Deism" of a Newton, Franklin or Jefferson today? I have rarely seen this very important question directly addressed though it is frequently indirectly addressed.

The 18th century Enlightenment stressed Reason, as is well-known. And this was done by Christians as well as non-Christians. In fact both believers and non-believers attempted to base their views on Reason.

For example, one of John Wesley's most famous sermons was called "An Earnest Appeal to Men of Reason and Religion." In a similar manner John Locke wrote an apologetic treatise called "The Reasonableness of Christianity." It seems quite clear as a general statement that Newton, Franklin, and Jefferson (all three) were trying to keep Christianity consistent with Reason and modern science, and because of this they not only de-emphasized the supernatural in the Bible, they tended to eliminate it entirely, and with some good Reason in the 18th century.

In the 18th century, it was a commonly held view that both the Old Testament as well as the New Testament were the product of "long oral tradition," or that is to say that both Testaments were written down only after their stories had been handed down orally **over many generations**. And it was held that the supernatural miracles had been added in as embellishments to the Bible stories over the many generations of oral transmission of both Testaments.

Though there is a theoretical if not practical possibility that this "long oral tradition" idea is true of the Old Testament, **it is actually theoretically impossible for the New Testament stories** about Jesus concerning the major supernatural events of the Virgin Birth and the Resurrection to be added in as embellishments. Why is this?

In the 18th century, it was widely assumed that the "historical Jesus" was *not* the Jesus of the Bible and that the stories of Jesus in the New Testament were not written down until the late second century in order to have "many generations" of "long oral tradition" pass before they were recorded.

However, by the end of the 19th century there was a general consensus that the Gospels were written down in the mid to late first century and that their stories are indeed the actual teachings and first-hand accounts of the Apostles, which means the major supernatural stories are true *or* the Apostles are making them up in a vast conspiracy, which is completely un-Reasonable.

Bottom line? By the end of the 19th century the "Deism" and "Christianity" of Newton, Franklin, and Jefferson become un-Reasonable because conspiracy theories are not Reasonable and because the **supernatural** intervention of God in history can indeed occur *if* there is a Creator God of Newton, Franklin, and Jefferson to do it. So, the Deism of Newton, Franklin, and Jefferson is going to merge into the Christianity of, say, a C. S. Lewis.

At the same time, by the mid 20th century the standard Deism of a clockwork universe where a God supposedly made everything and walked away is going to merge into an outright atheism, and these atheists will hold the universe is infinite and self-existent (a scientifically false fact) or that the universe created itself out of a self-generated big bang, which is also a non-scientific position.

This means by the mid 20th century due to Bible scholarship even by Higher Critics themselves, **the *only* Reasonable position** is the New Testament major stories are true, supernatural miracles and all. At the same time the atheists and Liberal Higher Critics openly degenerate into what is called **postmodernism** or, that is, **total irrationality** concerning not only the possibility of the supernatural but also into **total irrationality concerning all morality and all concepts of Justice, Righteousness, and the Higher Moral Law** of Jefferson and Franklin!!!

Thomas Jefferson on Justice, Virtue, and Good Government

At one point in 1793 Thomas Jefferson wrote of justice, virtue, and good government: "**All the tranquillity, the happiness & security of mankind rest on justice**, on the obligation to respect the rights of others." C. S. Lewis will express similar sentiments (famously) in the 20th century, but this could also be straight out of Augustine or Cicero of course, but still, it is pure Jefferson, regardless. Jefferson went on: "The respect of others for our rights of domain & property is the security of our actual possessions." (So much for Socialist Justice.)

In a similar manner, in 1801 in his First Inaugural Address, Jefferson held the **key to personal *and* civic virtues** is having "honesty, truth, temperance, gratitude and the love of man; [and] acknowledging and adoring an overruling Providence, which by all it's dispositions proves that it delights in the happiness of man here and his greater happiness hereafter." Jefferson, of course, means this *very* literally, *not* figuratively. He is *no* Liberal or atheist!

Jefferson then goes on to ask, "...what more is necessary to make us a happy and prosperous people? Still one thing more, fellow citizens, a wise and frugal Government, which shall restrain men from injuring one another, shall leave them otherwise free to regulate their own pursuits of industry and improvement, and shall not take from the mouths of labor **the bread it has earned**." This means for Jefferson our **modern Social Justice** that redistributes the fruits of one's labor to others would be the height of injustice! Hello, wake up, smell the coffee. Today's Democrat Party is overtly un-American and anti-Jefferson to its core.

Jefferson ends the above points by saying, "This is the sum of good government," that is, protecting property, pursuits of industry and the bread people have earned. And in doing this Jefferson says government has done what is "necessary to close the circle of our felicities."

The only questions then become what are Wise laws and regulations to these ends to be made by the true statesman, and what are Wise government undertakings and programs for the general well-being of the nation, and what are Wise and Just tax policies, etc.? And when any wealth redistribution is warranted, when and exactly how are we to do it, that is, if it is to be done in Wisdom, Justice, and Righteousness?

The School House, the Church House, and the Legislature
The school house and the church house have somewhat different functions in the society. People

go to church to worship God, to get their souls saved, to get right with God, and to receive Christ into their hearts for personal relationship. But that is not the function of the school or the state, according to Jefferson, generally correctly in my opinion.

One goes to school primarily to learn to read and write and to do mathematics and science and similar things and **to learn the desirability of moral virtue, and hence good citizenship, for the common good in Justice and Righteousness based on the moral Laws of Nature** as opposed to the foolishness of hedonism in one's personal life and special interest politics in government.

What is the bottom-line point? It is Jefferson and Franklin's famous point, namely, the practical application of Christ's moral teaching is what is important to the school house and to good government, and this is usually a separate issue than whether Christ died on the Cross for our sins or if He is the Second Person of the Trinity.

The humanists and Liberals are destroying education today because they want to get **Jesus out of the schools *because* of his moral teachings**, and it is the same reason they want to get Solomon as well as Isaiah, Socrates and Cicero **out of the schools**! But **for Jefferson** a central point, if not the central point, of good education and good government is to get Jesus ***into* the schools and government**. Hello, yet again, wake up and smell the coffee. Liberals and humanists use "separation of church and state" as a false, irrelevant, and ridiculous excuse for getting rid of **Jesus as a moral teacher** because they say he is worshipped in the Christian religion.

By contrast, today the great moral teachers such as Socrates and Cicero supposedly have to go because they are just "dead white men," Liberals frequently say. This is just yet another lame, irrelevant, and even racist excuse today to hide a **Liberal and humanist agenda** that rejects not only the very idea of God but of Justice and Righteousness in Wisdom, which in fact was the central point of good education and good government for Jefferson just as it had been from ancient times in Western civilization!

I think we should restore the tradition of giving all incoming Congressmen **Jefferson Bibles** of **the moral teachings of Jesus.** The book is actually entitled ***The Life and Morals of Jesus of Nazareth***. Jefferson did ***not*** presume to call it the Jefferson Bible. Regardless, Jefferson's Bible could ***also*** be a central text of moral virtue for the public schools as well. This way the youth will get a good education (according to Jefferson), and they will at the same time learn to understand principles of right living, truly happy living, and truly good government.

The Final Moral and Political Battle
The final moral and political battle for planet Earth will be between **two opposing "moral" worldviews on good and desirable government**. Will it be the

globalists' view of doing a *false* worldwide Social Justice with *false* human rights administered by an unelected world-governmental elite authority where there are few if any true rights for the individual, *or* will it be free and sovereign states with Liberty and Justice for all with equal *true* rights for all as expressed by Thomas Jefferson in the American Revolution of 1776 and by John Locke in the Glorious Revolution of 1688?

As Jefferson famously said, "We hold these Truths to be self-evident, that all Men are created equal, that they are endowed by their Creator with certain inalienable Rights, that among these are Life, Liberty, and the Pursuit of Happiness" or, that is one could say, the pursuit of *true* human fulfillment, and we know **for Jefferson** that true happiness and true fulfillment come from following **the moral teachings of Jesus**. Yet again, wake up and smell the coffee.

And as the Christian John Locke said before Jefferson, we have the God-given right to life, liberty, and property, and it is the purpose of good, right, and just government to protect those God-given rights, but this is not so for the person who rejects true and right individual liberty for collectivism and who rejects classical Justice and moral virtue for Social Justice and hedonism as today's Democrats do. Their opposing moral and political views and values to Locke and Jefferson create **the moral *and* political battles** of our time.

These battles are almost certainly **the final spiritual battle for planet Earth** of good against evil and against false light and false goods. The Bible is quite clear in countless prophecies that the forces of Locke and Jefferson will win with Liberty and Justice for all and that this victory will last a thousand years. Will it? No doubt time will tell if we are to win this battle in our time and if we are to continue the victory in the coming generations and centuries.

However, this victory can *only* be secured at the ballot box by voting against *all* Democrat candidates with their Social Justice agenda and its false moral and false agape love notions that stand *against* everything that Jefferson believed in and gave his life to. And what did Jefferson believe in as the point of life and good government and as the cause of true happiness and true fulfillment? The answer is classical Justice and Righteousness taught by Jesus, as we have already seen.

Justice and Righteousness
The Two Great Commandments of love God with all your heart, mind and soul, and love your neighbor as yourself are not only central to Jefferson's theory of true human happiness, right living, and good government, they are foundational to classical concepts of Justice and Righteousness.

The Bible talks of the Justice and Righteousness combo over sixty times in some translations. I tend to capitalize the terms because I am something of a

Platonist. Not only are Justice and Righteousness very real and objective things, they are also very real attributes and defining qualities of God.

Discussing Justice and Righteousness can be something of a daunting task in our time for a variety of reasons, but, in truth, Justice and Righteousness are actually central themes in the philosophy of Plato, Aristotle, and Cicero as well as in the Bible and in antiquity in the great Saint Augustine and in modern times in the writings of John Locke as well as Thomas Jefferson.

So, Justice and Righteousness are central themes of the Bible, Western civilization, and the major figures of Greco-Roman philosophy as well as central themes of major Christian writers and all good social political philosophers of modernity, but tragically today few people know much about any of this. Even the most basic elements of the topic of Justice and Righteousness have been lost in our time. There is a reason for this.

Cicero and Locke
In the late 19th century, atheists and Liberals came to hold that classical Justice and Righteousness as well as God (or God as traditionally understood) are either bad things or do not exist at all, and so classical education, the Bible, and central figures dealing with Justice and Righteousness, such as **Cicero and Locke** in particular, were consciously taken out of the education curriculum. At the same

time atheists and Liberals distorted the teachings and beliefs of Thomas Jefferson, as we have seen.

Where Cicero and Locke had been central to a good education as well as important and central figures in the Glorious Revolution and the American Revolution, in the late 19th century they were attacked and/or removed from education, and generally this meant the moral Natural Law or what Jefferson called the moral "Laws of Nature and of Nature's God" had to go as well.

This means if someone went to most colleges throughout the 20th century, there would be little said or good said about such figures as Cicero or Locke or about the topic of Justice and Righteousness or about the topic of the Natural Law. The renowned British scholar Michael Grant speaks of this, and he thinks it is a bad thing and he laments it. The famous atheist-agnostic Bertrand Russell speaks of it as well, and he thinks it is a very good thing, and he celebrates it as a *supposed* progress of the UK, the US, and even of mankind and Western civilization!

However, nature abhors a vacuum, and into the void left by the removal of classical teachings on Justice and Righteousness rush the related opposite positions of **Socialist Justice and hedonism**, which were actually constructed to be **the opposites of classical Justice and Righteousness**. However, these things are little known facts today.

In fact, so devoid is education of teachings on Justice and Righteousness that many well-meaning people actually hold that when the Bible speaks of Justice and Righteousness, it actually means Social Justice or, that is, non-violent communism. Though this is much outrageous silliness, incredibly such prominent Christian teachers as Timothy Keller actually hold this view.

On the other hand, C. S. Lewis held that it is the devil, quite literally, who wants you to think that Social Justice is a good thing (and not an evil thing) and not only that but Social Justice is the point of the Christian faith and **not** classical Justice and Righteousness or, in essence, that is, the Two Great Commandments of Jesus and Jefferson.

Apparently the highly esteemed Mr. Keller did not read his Lewis too carefully nor get a good classical education, which is certainly **not** his fault since few if any people did get a classical education in the 20th century and especially in the late 20th century. Allan Bloom decried this situation in his must-read book *The Closing of the American Mind*, but in that book even Bloom is not able to reconstruct classical concepts of Justice and Righteousness.

Justice and Righteousness, the basics
What are the basics of Justice and Righteousness as developed for Western civilization in the ancient Greco-Roman philosophy of Plato, Aristotle, and Cicero? This is a very important question, not just

generally for right living and good government, but also for reading the Bible because when the Bible speaks of Justice and Righteousness, it is generally *not* speaking of the Law of Moses, but rather it is speaking of common sense notions of Justice and Righteousness and about natural-theology and natural-philosophy meanings of the terms Justice and Righteousness.

This means without a good classical education it is very difficult to read the Bible and the Old Testament in particular because it was in ancient Athens that a systematic and even definitive treatment of the ideas of **Justice and Righteousness were worked out for Western civilization and for all time**.

Would you like the story of Justice and Righteousness in a single sentence as worked out by Socrates, Plato, and Aristotle? If so, here it is: **When the individual practices moral virtue, that is doing Righteousness, and when the state does moral virtue, that is doing Justice**. Righteousness is for the individual what Justice is for the state. Simple enough.

Moral Virtue and Self-Interest
Moral virtue is doing the right thing in relationship to human interaction. However, not all right actions have to do with morality, as such. For example, **non-moral practical pragmatism** is just doing what is appropriate or right given some ends, such as doing

the right or proper thing, say, to fix an automobile. However, doing the right thing in human interaction deals with the moral.

Doing "the Right thing" morally speaking in relationship to others is practicing the Second Great Commandment (love your neighbor as yourself) **or doing the Golden Rule** (do unto others as you would have them do unto you). The Golden Rule is a slightly different formulation of the Second Great Commandment as a general principle for morally right human interaction.

The central question of Plato's *Republic* and of Aristotle's *Nicomachean Ethics* and of Cicero's *On Duties* is one and the same, namely, **is doing the morally right thing in one's *true* self-interest?** And in slightly different form this is the main question of Solomon's Proverbs in the Bible, namely, what is the practical Wisdom or desirability of doing the morally right thing?

Socrates in Plato's *Republic* asserts that it is *always* in one's *true* **self-interest** to do the morally right thing, and it is *never* in one's true self-interest to do an immoral action (as, say, stealing something).

Socrates holds that morally right actions are *always* to one's benefit in the long run, and *if* one does not get a benefit from moral action in this life, one will get a reward by God in the next life. After Plato further develops this idea, Aristotle and Cicero will argue that not only does one's *true* self-interest for personal gain lie in doing the morally right thing, but if one thinks an immoral action (such as stealing, false witness, etc.) will bring desirable gain, that in itself proves one is not thinking straight!

The importance for us today of these lost truths of Western civilization and of the Bible cannot be overstated. In classical moral theory as well as in plain common sense there is, on the one hand, **a moral, mutual or legitimate self-interest, *and*** there is, on the other hand, **an immoral, selfish, or illegitimate self-interest,** and the point of **Right living, Right Reason and Wisdom is to figure out which is which in any given situation**, but not so for the Liberal, the communist, the socialist, and the atheist, all of whom do *not* believe in the moral Laws of Nature and of Nature's God of Jefferson, Locke, and Cicero. For the Liberal, the communist, the socialist, and the atheist moral virtue or Right living and Right Reason are *not* the point of life or of the Christian faith. In fact, they do not exist at all!

For the atheist, Epicurean and fool, hedonism and self-indulgence are the point of life. For the socialist, communist and Liberal, any and *all* **self-interest** is supposedly an evil and is, therefore, "immoral" and selfish. (Read their works!) ***Only* working for the collective** or doing what the Liberals call agape, self-sacrificial love is a good, and all else is an evil! This is why in communist and socialist systems the new so-called "socialist man" *only* desires to work *for* the collective and *not* for himself, and in Marxist Leninism he must do so at the point of a gun! This is a **dehumanizing communist dystopia**.

By contrast, in a **utopian** Social-Justice communism, the new socialist man as well as the supposedly true Christian does all work for the collective for **free** *and* **voluntarily** and for **no personal gain** at all, and if one does not feel like working at any job, one just stays at home and watches TV all day or one goes out and parties all day **while one collects one's equal share of the society's wealth** to be handed out to everyone equally as a positive Social-Justice basic "human right," whether one works or not.

This utopian Socialist Justice of non-violent communism (of Social Democrats) is all utterly ridiculous of course and outrageously so, but it is quite the vogue in most of our schools and churches, and it has been at least since the end of World War II with the Social-Justice founding of *both* the United Nations *and* the World Council of Churches.

However, **for the Bible, Western civilization and just plain common sense more generally, the point of life is moral, mutual or legitimate self-interest, and such harmonious interaction of all people in the society by the Golden Rule creates the Just society of the commonwealth, and in economic activities it creates the wealth of the nation, says Adam Smith correctly**.

The duty of the good legislator, called a statesman, is, as Jefferson said, to make good laws to facilitate the Justice of this overall harmonious and mutually beneficial interaction and to punish people who try to exploit others in improper, immoral or selfish interaction, such as in stealing or fraud, etc. And the statesman needs the Wisdom (of God) to do the morally right thing for good of the society in making such Good or Right legislation. And, as Franklin said, he or she should pray for such Wisdom.

Bottom line: The atheist, the Liberal, the communist, the Social Justice Warrior, and hence **all Democrats and Labour Party members** and all socialist democrats generally are clueless and generally utopian concerning true Right living, Righteousness, moral virtue, true self-interest, and true agape love, let alone wrong and clueless about capitalism, good economics, individual rights, free enterprise, and the wealth of the nation. The Liberals literally get virtually **nothing** right, and this is no small accomplishment if you stop and think about it!

The Moral and the Practical
Right living or Wise living is about doing **the moral** and **the practical**. Again, doing the moral and the practical is in one's *true* **self-interest**, and this is *not* a selfish or immoral self-interest says Cicero as the main point of his philosophy in *On Duties* and so says Solomon, in effect, as the main point of the book of Proverbs, most of which was written or compiled by Solomon.

This is all about doing personal Righteousness, but in point of fact **the moral** and **the practical** are also the point of Good or Just legislation says Cicero, and Ronald Reagan said **the moral** and **the practical** combo was the essence of the Reagan Revolution. Rather obviously, Reagan had a good classical education and had been reading his Cicero.

In something of a related manner, C. S. Lewis correctly said the good society cannot merely be legislated. The harmonious interaction of all the parts of the body politic is dependent upon each person attempting to practice the Golden Rule (that is, moral virtue) in all that he does.

There is no shortcut to the good society Lewis says. On this matter, Lewis says famously, "the longest way around [by getting each person on board for the Golden Rule] is the shortest way home" to the good society. Do the math here, folks, on what we need to be teaching in our schools, namely, classical teachings on Justice and Righteousness, moral virtue, and the whole point of the Jewish and Christian life, namely, the Two Great Commandments of the Old and New Testaments. This is all just as Jefferson said.

The Two Great Commandments
Jesus said, correctly in my opinion, the entire point of Judaism is to practice the Two Great Commandments (love God with all your heart, mind and soul, and love your neighbor as yourself), and if

this is so, it certainly does not change for Christianity. This is so simple that a child can understand it and so deep and profound that one can never plunge the depths of it, but the devil comes to kill, rob, and destroy.

The devil wants to sow seeds of bitterness, hate and resentment and wrongful self-advantage and a self-based life that seeks its own power, pleasure, fame or fortune, as ends in themselves or at the expense of others or as gods in themselves, as it were. There is no inherent evil in power, pleasure, fame or fortune, but they are not the point of life nor is a self-based life or self-first over moral good. We are to have a God or Good based life, and hence the First Great Commandment, and hence, then the Second Great Commandment is to love our neighbor as our self.

The devil has self-advantage *over* others as the basis of life, which for its part for ill-gotten gain uses hate, manipulation, exploitation, resentment, deception, etc. These things are clear evils in classical moral theory. When the devil is unsuccessful sowing these outright evils (let not the sun go down on your anger lest you give place to the devil and develop a root of bitterness), **he will sow false goods as true goods**.

The three most common false goods in the church today are, 1.) **agape love as (moral) lawlessness** (which is pure Gnosticism), 2.) **agape love as "unconditional love" or acceptance** (universalism or all go to heaven) and, 3.) **agape love as selfless or**

utopian self-sacrificial service where anything that is selfless is good and anything that is not an altruistic selfless charity is supposedly selfish and evil. Apostate Christian Liberalism generally falls for all three of these as demonic substitutes for the Second Great Commandment or Golden Rule.

Social Justice is the devil's "Justice." The Social Gospel is the devil's "Gospel." Unconditional love is the devil's "love," and utopian selfless service (of the new socialist man) is the devil's moral virtue. The importance of this cannot be overstated. The point of the Second Great Commandment is the moral virtue of treating others as ourselves or as we would wish to be treated. The Second Great Commandment does *not* say to go out and do selfless service to others all day with no self-interest. There are, no doubt, times when we should do things for others with no self-interest, but this is not the general rule of moral virtue. Though some exceptional people do in fact have the spiritual gift of mercy, this is not the general condition of mankind.

The story of the Good Samaritan comes to mind here as does the story where Jesus said, "So much as you did it unto the least of them you did it unto me." However, the point of these stories of self-sacrificial love is *if* you were robbed and beaten up and left on the side of the road, you would want someone to be a Good Samaritan to you! Or *if* you were in prison, naked or hungry, etc., you would want someone to do selfless service to you!

Quite simply, there are moral situations where the Golden Rule and Second Great Commandment call for totally selfless service, but these situations are the exception rather than the rule, and totally selfless service as the *only* good means one would not even get a paycheck for one's work, which is **the central point of communism and of Socialist Justice** where one works all day for the collective for no pay or for only subsistence wages. But this would be, of course, an actual injustice. This is why Social Justice is the devil's "Justice." Never forget that working for a paycheck, free enterprise, private property, capitalism, and virtually *all* traditional rights of the individual are evils for the communist, socialist or collectivist **as the centerpiece and foundational point** of his collectivism, and they are evils based on his single false "moral" standard of utopian selfless service and self-last, etc., as supposedly the *only* good "moral" standard.

Defining Justice, Righteousness, and Salvation
Justice has various **definitions** in classical literature and in common sense, such as getting one's appropriate due, treating equals equally, getting the fruits of one's labors, and the harmonious interaction of all the parts of the body politic or commonwealth.

As Jefferson held the **statesman tries to see these interrelated notions of Justice** happen in the general society with good legislation, but for each of us **individually in order to have *true* happiness**

and fulfillment we are (as Jefferson also said) to live in moral **Righteousness,** which is basically the Second Great Commandment or Golden Rule, and generally this involves a certain reciprocity.

Further, **we are under a moral imperative by God by overt commandment as well as by the moral Natural Law to live by the Golden Rule** whether others are living by it or not. The Second Great Commandment does not say do utopian selfless service all day *nor* does it say to love your neighbor as yourself *only* if he is loving you as himself!

Simply stated, **practicing the Two Great Commandments *is* following Jesus, as Jefferson says.** However, this is *not* Christian salvation, which is all have sinned and fallen short of the glory of God and need a Savior to be made right with God and to have a **personal Abba Father relationship** with the Creator of the entire universe and everything in it.

Further, as Franklin realized one needs an anointing specifically from the one true God of Abraham, Issac and Jacob in order to do *true* **statesmanship**, and hence, we should seek this divine guidance in prayer in order to avoid the *1984* foolishness of the EU and UN as advocated by the Liberal and Gnostic.

Bottom line: Statesmanship does Justice and Righteousness for the common good as the right thing for the nation as a whole or commonwealth, while Christian salvation is accepting the atoning work of Christ for one's self personally in order to have the Abba Father relationship with our Creator.

Seek ye first the Kingdom
The Two Great Commandments are repeated in Scripture in various forms. When Jesus said, (Matthew 6:33-34) "Seek ye first the kingdom of God, and his Righteousness; and all these things shall be added unto you. Take therefore no thought for the morrow: for the morrow shall take thought for the things of itself. Sufficient unto the day is the evil thereof." Here we see basically the Two Great Commandments. The Kingdom of God is essentially wherever the Spirit of God reigns, and this is what we are to seek first in life (and not self-advantage). This is just as the First Great Commandment to love God with all your heart, mind, and soul.

Second, we are to "seek" the Righteousness of God or His Kingdom. Again, this is not very complicated. And this is just as the Second Great Commandment to love your neighbor as yourself, **and** in Christianity it is to accept our Righteousness in Christ by his atoning work. Further, as we live Rightly or Wisely in moral virtue, we tend naturally to have the things we need in life come to us **and** we tend to have the blessings of God upon us as well. This is, in essence, the point of the book of Proverbs and of **true** self-interest.

By contrast, a man once asked a Social Justice Warrior who was a pastor about right living and moral virtue as central to solving the world's poverty problems, and the pastor explained to the inquirer that right living and moral virtue were simply false middle class values of capitalism and that world poverty would *only* be solved by a world government doing worldwide Social Justice to alleviate all poverty by redistributing all the wealth of the world equally to everyone whether they work or not. How wrong and confused that pastor was!

Deny self and follow me
Jesus said (Matthew 16:24) "If any man will come after me, let him deny himself, and take up his cross, and follow me." **Again, we see the Two Great Commandments of Jesus and Jefferson.** First, do not have a self-based life but a God or Good based life in loving God with all one's heart, mind and soul, and second, we are to follow Christ in moral virtue and its agape love. As a famous Gospel song says, "Do your duty, never fail." In Romans 13 Paul even says outright **that moral virtue is loving your neighbor as yourself *and* that this is the point of agape love**, and primarily it is doing your neighbor no harm, which is, implicitly, as you would want done to you (and it is *not* doing selfless service to him all day as the Liberal utopian holds).

C. S. Lewis is one of the few writers I know of who really analyzes this. He says men tend to think in terms of doing no harm as a moral good, just as Paul says in Romans 13. Interestingly, Lewis says women by nature tend to process the Golden Rule (for their part) in terms of small acts of kindness, compassion, and service as a moral norm of life in a way that men simply do not do. This strikes me as a very astute observation by Lewis, but the general point of Jesus remains. The Two Great Commandments (say Jesus and Jefferson) sum up the entire point of Scripture for both Judaism and Christianity.

In Summary: Christianity, the Two Great Commandments, and Good Government
What Christianity adds to Judaism is the perfect and complete reconciliation to God in the atoning work of Christ, and by **accepting this atoning work** for one's self, one has an **assurance of heaven** and one gets **a born-again new heart** to God as well as **the indwelling Holy Spirit in personal experience** that gives a peace that passes all understanding and that gives, for human brings on Earth, **an Abba Father relationship** to the Creator of the entire universe.

And of this Lewis says it is possible that this relationship is the whole reason God created the universe and everything in it! Again, this strikes me as a pretty profound insight and possibility. God made us and the entire universe to the ends of us having intimate spiritual fellowship with Him and in Christ specifically. This is enough to leave one speechless where there is nothing left to do but sing praises and thanksgiving to God.

Still, **the moral virtue point of the Second Great Commandment remains**. As Paul said (2 Timothy

3:16-17), "All scripture is given by inspiration of God, and is profitable for doctrine, for reproof, for correction, **for instruction in righteousness**: That the man of God may be perfect, thoroughly furnished **unto all good works**." And similarly Peter says, Christ died for our sins that we may be dead to sin and "live unto righteousness." (1 Peter 2:24)

Jesus had said all Scripture is summarized by the Two Great Commandments, and Paul says all Scripture is given for the truth of Right doctrine and for Right living in moral virtue or Righteousness so that we can be made perfectly complete and mature in good works as individuals (and not be in immoral self-advantage or in hedonistic works of sin).

As statesmen or merely as voters we are **to pray as Solomon did that we will have the Wisdom of God to do Justice in good government *or* in good voting** and not the injustice of Social Justice and similar things of today's Democrat Party in the US and Labour Party in the UK.

The response to this is often, "But what of the Christian duty of helping the poor?" The answer is classical Justice deals with this in treating equals equally and helping those in true need as we would want done to us. This is known in our time by the saying "a safety net not a hammock."

Social Justice says we all deserve a hammock as a "positive right" by virtue of our humanity and whether we work or not! Classical Justice says provision should be made to help people in true need, and it should treat people the same in the same need. This, indeed, involves some limited wealth redistribution, Wisely done, but wealth redistribution is not the main point of the **Just state** as it is in the **Social Justice state**.

A true concept of Justice is in the law of Moses, *and* it is in natural philosophical concepts, *and* it is even written into the US Constitution that one of the main purposes of the United States government is to "establish Justice." This means it is not, as some argue, inherently un-Constitutional to have various safety net programs, provisions or national projects.

Conclusion

So, the end goal of good government? **One nation under God with Liberty and Justice for all and with consent of the governed and with equal rights for all based on the moral Laws of Nature and of Nature's God, Wisely applied for the common good or general welfare by the statesman legislator.**

When you get right down to it, Justice and Righteousness of the Bible and natural philosophy are pretty straightforward though particular applications can require the Wisdom of Solomon, which is Christ Himself in us, says Proverbs 8. And, indeed, Christ is said to rule and reign in and through the saints in doing Justice and Righteousness in good government throughout the world in the much prophesied millennial Kingdom Era to come.

Romans 13:10b says that **agape "love is the fulfillment of the law" of Moses**, concerning putting God first and loving our neighbors as ourselves. This is moral virtue and our *true* self-interest, and if we do not get our rewards in this life, we will in the next, as Plato, Cicero, Jesus, and even Thomas Jefferson said.

Someone once said that all our problems in life and in doing good government could be solved if all people in general and all people in government in particular lived by the simple maxim,"Do the Right thing."

Indeed, in classical philosophy this is called using Right Reason (Logos-Christology), and it practices the four cardinal virtues of Justice, moderation (temperance), discernment (prudence), and courage (fortitude). The three specifically Christian virtues are, of course, said to be "faith, hope, and love" and "the greatest of these is love."

Postscript: Three strikes and you're out
For the Democrats, three strikes and you're out. What are the three strikes? Strike one, Ted Kennedy and the Democrats' *successful* outrageous and disgraceful character assassination of Robert Bork on what appeared to be completely baseless and unsubstantiated charges.

This was a game-changer in history for the Left and for the false "living" Constitution of the Democrats, who believe in the absurd *1984* notion that the Constitution can live to mean virtually anything on the Leftist political agenda, even **the opposite** of original intent! This is all explained in detail by Robert Bork in his landmark book *The Tempting of America: The Political Seduction of the Law.*

That book combined with his *Slouching Towards Gomorrah: Modern Liberalism and American Decline* will stand as something of a definitive treatment of American Constitutional law and of the American culture more generally for generations and even centuries to come. The impact of Bork's two books could become unequaled in American history, and they will presumably be central in the restoration of our constitutional Republic.

However, these two books in all likelihood would never have been written if Bork had been confirmed to the Court. God works in mysterious ways His wonders to perform. What is most interesting is during all of this the brilliant Bork actually held a very quirky view of no judicial review, which in itself could have been legitimate grounds not to confirm him to the Court rather than doing the character assassination as the Democrats did.

Some few years later came strike two, which was Anita Hill and the Democrats' **unsuccessful** outrageous and disgraceful character assassination of

Clarence Thomas *also* done on what appeared to be completely baseless and unsubstantiated charges.

Clarence Thomas is a great champion of civil rights in our time, and the Democrats will never live down turning on him as they did simply because of his race. In so turning on him they passed the ball of defending true civil rights in the legacy of Martin Luther King to the Republicans, the political party established by Abraham Lincoln, no less.

And now in the past few weeks comes strike three, which is Christine Blasey Ford and the Democrats' shameful character assassination of Brett Kavanaugh, yet again on what appeared to be almost completely baseless and unsubstantiated charges, and in doing this they were often in complete and flagrant violation of Senate rules concerning the confirmation process, time and again. Outrageous.

It is inconceivable to me that any American can ever again vote for any Democrat under almost any circumstances. Today's Democrat Party has generally become practically un-American, blatantly anti-Jeffersonian, and openly un-Constitutional. The clear intent as well as the rules and procedures of the Constitution have been thrown to the wind for political purposes since the Bork disaster. This sad state of affairs with today's Democrats is the greatest scandal in American political history. In fact, this is arguably the greatest scandal in world political history, no small feat by the Democrats.

Other booklets on the Reign of Christ in this
UNDERSTANDING Series:

UNDERSTANDING Prophecy Fulfillment:
The Great Apostasy, Babylon, Mystery Babylon & the Reign of Christ

This little booklet gives an overview of the central major prophecies concerning the possible soon coming Reign of Christ. Specifically these are the prophecies of the Great Apostasy, Babylon, Mystery Babylon, and the man of lawlessness. These prophecies are seen as fulfilled in the false millennial visions of Marx and of the New World Order of UN Agenda 21 and Agenda 2030 and in the Liberal World Council of Churches.

UNDERSTANDING All Bible Prophecy:
Genesis to Revelation

This booklet holds that all prophecy should be interpreted in terms of the larger story of the Bible and the larger story of the Christian cosmology from the Creation to the Final Judgment, and this is especially the case for the book of Revelation.

UNDERSTANDING Globalism:
What is the "New World Order"?

This booklet looks at what "globalism" is generally and at the related topic of a "New World Order" that actually has *very* specific definitions and formulations that are often not well-known.

UNDERSTANDING Revelation 19:
Victory over One-World Government and One-World Religion

Revelation 19 though very controversial is actually very straightforward. The saints in a Marriage Supper of the Lamb move into a new more mature, intimate, and complete relationship with Christ, and then the saints in Christ and Christ in the saints completely and totally defeat the evils of one-world government and one-world religion. Simple enough when you get right down to it.

UNDERSTANDING Statesmanship
Classical Justice *versus* Social Justice

Probably no two notions are more misunderstood as well as more necessary to understand in our time than classical Justice and Social Justice. This booklet looks at the history of these two terms and how one stands for the Justice of statesmanship for doing the common good and the other for the injustice of special interest groups and wealth redistribution as a false human right for economic equality.

UNDERSTANDING Alternative Political Universes:
The Natural Revelation & Self-Evident Truths

For some folks as Jefferson and the American founders, the Natural Law or so-called Higher Moral Law is a self-evident truth, but for others with a reprobate mind and no common sense, this is not the case at all. These modern-day people who have lost their common sense are just as the ancient Epicureans (atheist hedonists) while modern-day Liberals are just as ancient Gnostics with their false enlightenment and false morality. Understand these things, and you will pretty well understand Alternative Political Universes.

UNDERSTANDING Illegal Immigration:
The Wall and All It Stands For

"The Wall" of Donald Trump stands for many larger issues from exposing hypocrisy among professional politicians to ending globalism, open borders, and the often total lawlessness of our time. Lawlessness of the Liberal and atheist-humanist is, in fact, the spirit of anti-Christ.

UNDERSTANDING The Whole Counsel of the Kingdom:
The Central Message of Jesus and Paul

Both Jesus and Paul preached a Whole Counsel of the Kingdom message, but this is not a generally well-known truth. This booklet looks at the concept of a Whole Counsel of the Kingdom Christianity and what it entails, namely, true worship of God in Spirit and Truth as well as Just and Righteous government.

UNDERSTANDING Spiritual Warfare:
Satan as a Roaring Lion

Scripture tells us that Satan goes about like a roaring lion seeking whom he may devour, but this is generally not a very understood warning, and tragically many people, if not devoured completely, get an arm or leg eaten (so to speak). To be forewarned is to be forearmed. This booklet deals with ways to recognize and deal with demons.

===

All of the above booklets are part of a series on key issues of our time on the Reign of Christ at
www.ashiningcityonahill.org
www.reignofchrist.org

All of the above booklets are put together in a single **Volume I** called

UNDERSTANDING
The Reign of CHRIST:
The One Big Issue of Our Time
Volume I

This Volume I of all the above booklets together as well as all of the above booklets separately are available at **amazon.com**